Cats and Kittens

Katherine Starke

🐾

Designed by Kathy Ward
Edited by Fiona Watt

🐾

Illustrated by Christyan Fox
Photographs by Jane Burton
Cover design by Amanda Gulliver
Additional research by Jonathan Sheikh-Miller

CONTENTS

With additional photographs by Howard Allman
Consultant: Sarah Hartwell
With thanks to Andrew Kirby

Choosing a kitten

If you are thinking of getting your first cat, it's a good idea to get a kitten. A kitten needs more care to start with but may find it easier to fit into a new home. Before choosing, try to visit different families of kittens to find one that you like.

Types of cats

Some people breed cats so that they have special mixtures of fur shades and length. These cats are called purebred.
Most cats are a mixture of breeds.

Where to start

If you get two kittens they will keep each other company.

Nearly all ginger cats, like this one, are male.

If you choose a long-haired kitten, it will need to be brushed more often than one with short hair.

Ask friends if they know anyone whose cat has had kittens. Local vets and animal shelters are a good place to ask too.

This brown and white kitten is called a tabby. It is a mixture of different breeds.

At 8-12 weeks old a kitten will be ready to leave its mother. A kitten learns from its mother and from playing with the other kittens in its family.

For links to websites, go to
www.usborne-quicklinks.com
and enter the keywords "first pets cats".

Which one?

A fluffy kitten will probably grow up to be a fluffy cat.

Choose one which you think will suit you.

Play with the kittens before you choose one.

Find out about the kittens' mother if you can. Her kittens may grow up to look like her or the father.

Watch the kittens to find out what they are like. Some kittens are quiet and others are more active.

Choose a kitten that's lively but not aggressive. Ask the owners if they have noticed how your kitten behaves.

Ancient pets

The Egyptian word for cat is "mau".

Cats have been kept as pets for thousands of years. It is thought that the first people to keep cats in their homes were the Ancient Egyptians, about 5000 years ago.

Wild things

Your cat may behave like a wild cat. Leopards lie like this in long grass.

Tame cats, like yours, are called domestic cats. Domestic cats are related to wild cats such as lions, cheetahs and leopards. Your cat may behave like a wild cat at times.

What will I need?

You will need to get some special things to help you to look after your cat. Make sure you have everything ready for your new kitten or cat before you bring it home.

Pet carrier

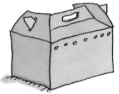

Buy a carrier from a vet or a pet store.

You will need a special pet carrier to take your cat home. An ordinary cardboard box is not safe or strong enough.

Toys

Cats often play hunting games with their toys.

You can buy toy animals and balls from a pet store.

Your cat will need some toys so that it doesn't get bored. Never leave yarn or string with your cat. It could choke on it.

Cats like things that can roll around or move easily. You could make some toys for your cat - see pages 12-13 for some ideas.

Litter tray

Put the litter tray on newspaper to keep the floor clean.

Inside your house, your cat can go to the toilet in a litter tray, also called a litter box. Buy a plastic tray and special grit, called cat litter.

Food

Make sure the food has the word 'complete' on the label.

KITTYLIX

CHICK

Use saucers or small bowls for food dishes.

You will also need some food. Canned or dry food is the easiest to use. Buy just one or two cans at first in case your cat doesn't like it.

Choose food dishes with shallow sides so that your cat can reach inside. Have one dish for food and one dish for water.

For links to websites, go to
www.usborne-quicklinks.com
and enter the keywords "first pets cats".

Make a bed

Put newspapers under the bed to lift it away from the cold floor.

Find a large cardboard box, about twice the size of your cat. Cut off any flaps at the top. Carefully cut a section out of one side, about 5cm (2in) from the edges.

Put newspapers in the bottom and around the sides of the box. Fold up an old sweater or blanket. Put this in the bottom of the box to make a comfortable bed.

Just the place

Cats like to have their food dishes, their litter tray and their bed in separate places. Try to find places for all these where it is quiet and your cat will not be disturbed.

DO NOT DISTURB

Put your cat's bed in a warm, quiet place.

First steps

It will take some time for your cat to get used to all the different sights and smells in your home. Keep your cat in just one or two rooms for the first two or three days.

Show your cat its food, litter tray and bed by tapping them gently and calling its name. Make sure it can always get to these things when it needs to.

Warm welcome

Talk to your cat quietly to get it used to your voice.

Open the pet carrier and let your cat look around. Tip the carrier very gently so that it can climb out.

Let your cat explore without picking it up. Stay still and let your cat explore you as well.

When it feels at home your cat may start to wash itself. This shows that your cat thinks it is in a safe place.

Introducing yourself

Get your cat's attention by calling its name. It is more likely to come to you if you crouch down and are still. Some cats can be very shy at first.

Your cat could be very nervous and may creep up to you slowly.

Hold out your hand so that your cat can sniff your fingers.

For links to websites, go to
www.usborne-quicklinks.com
and enter the keywords "first pets cats".

Stroking your cat

Stroke your cat gently around its ears and under its chin.

Most cats don't like their stomach to be touched.

Most cats like to be stroked. Stroking may remind your cat of its mother licking it clean. Smooth its fur down gently in the direction that it grows.

Your cat might sit on your lap to be stroked. If it feels happy, your cat may knead you with its paws. Kittens knead their mother when they want milk.

Smells like home

Your cat might rub its head against you, too.

Your cat rubs its head against things to mix its smell with objects and people. This makes places seem less strange to it.

Territory

Cats often share parts of a territory.

A cat usually has an area that it treats as its own. This is called its territory. Cats mark their territory by spraying and rubbing with their scent, and scratching things.

Settling in

Most cats like to be stroked and cuddled, but make sure your cat knows you are there, before you pick it up. Get your kitten used to being handled and meeting other pets while it is still young. Keep other pets away from your cat for at least a day. It is best never to let a cat or kitten meet small pets such as mice, rabbits or birds.

Holding your cat

Talk quietly to your cat to keep it calm.

It may scratch you if it doesn't want to be held.

Use both hands to pick your cat up. Lift it with one hand under its chest. Gather up its back legs.

Hold your cat against your chest so that it feels safe. Support it with one hand under its back legs.

If it struggles, put your cat onto the floor very gently. Let it go when its feet are on the ground.

The first night

It will be used to feeling warm with its mother.

When two cats meet, they both put their tails straight up. This a greeting sign.

A kitten may meow a lot when it is left on its own. Wrap a hot water bottle in a towel and put it in its bed.

For links to websites, go to
www.usborne-quicklinks.com
and enter the keywords "first pets cats".

Meeting other pets

Before your pets meet, exchange a piece of bedding from each of their beds. This will mix their smells. Have someone with you when your pets meet so that you can make a fuss of both of your pets. As your pets get used to each other, your cat will start to feel as if it is part of the same family.

*Put their bowls
a little way
away from
each other.*

*Always stay
with your pets
for the first few
meetings.*

Let your pets meet before a meal. They will probably be more interested in their food than in each other.

If your other pet is a dog, keep it on a leash for the first few meetings. Keep the meeting quite short.

*If one of your pets
tries to fight, pick
the other one up.*

*Let both of
your pets sniff
each other.*

Feeding

Cats need to eat meat to stay healthy. In the wild, your cat would eat small animals such as mice, rabbits and rats. It would also eat birds and fish. A lot of cats like cows' milk, but it can give them an upset stomach. Only give your cat milk occasionally.

Cats like to be left alone when they eat.

If you have two cats, give them separate bowls.

Feeding your cat

mEOW!

Your cat might meow when it is hungry. Feed your cat at the same times each day.

Put one tablespoon into the bowl.

Up to four months old, feed your kitten four or five small meals a day. This is better than two big meals.

Fill a different dish with cold water. Make sure there is always fresh water in your cat's dish.

As your kitten gets older, feed it fewer but larger meals.

At six months old, cut down to 2 or 3 meals a day. Each meal should be about 4 spoons of canned food.

For links to websites, go to
www.usborne-quicklinks.com
and enter the keywords "first pets cats".

Dry foods

You can give your cat dry food instead of canned food if you like. Crunching on dry food helps to keep your cat's teeth clean. Don't mix dry food with other food or it will get soggy.

Your cat will drink more water with dry food.

Always wash the bowl when your cat has finished eating.

Teeth and tongue

Cats have small back teeth for chewing meat.

mEOW!

A cat's front teeth are for biting food.

A cat uses its tongue like a spoon, to lap up water.

At six months old, kittens lose their first teeth and grow adult ones. Although cats' teeth are very sharp and good at biting, they cannot chew food as well as you can.

A cat's tongue is covered with tiny hooks which make it very rough. The hooks are useful for cleaning fur and, in the wild, for tearing meat off bones.

Playing

Cats and kittens love to play. They like toys which they can roll around and pounce on. Cats like to climb inside boxes and paper bags. Keep plastic bags away from your cat - it could suffocate in one.

Why do cats play?

A mother cat will twitch her tail for her kittens to chase.

Cats mainly play to exercise, but also to learn how to hunt (see pages 26-27). They're also very inquisitive and like to explore new things.

Kittens love climbing on things so they can see all around them.

These kittens are playing in a kitten playhouse.

For links to websites, go to
www.usborne-quicklinks.com
and enter the keywords "first pets cats".

Make a playhouse

Bend the flaps out of the box.

Draw one circle on a flap.

1. Find a cardboard box bigger than your kitten. Make sure the box has four flaps at the top.

2. Draw circles of different sizes on the box. Make some bigger and some smaller than your kitten.

3. Get someone to help you cut out the circles with a bread knife. Tape the flaps together firmly.

Kitten games

Watch how your kitten plays different games with its toys. It may pretend it is catching a bird by throwing a toy up in the air. Kittens of wild cats do this too. A mother cheetah will bring small animals back for her kittens to play with.

Watch out for claws

Your kitten might grab you with its claws when you are playing with it. Calm it down by talking to it quietly. Take your hand away slowly.

This kitten's tail is pointing up to show it is happy.

This kitten is pretending to catch a mouse and has grabbed its toy with its claws.

13

Fur

Fur protects your cat's skin and helps to keep it warm, just as your clothes protect you. Cats keep their fur clean by licking it with their rough tongues.

Shedding

Cats shed some of their fur all the time. Old hairs fall out and are replaced by new hairs. Their fur also grows thicker to keep them warm during the winter. In the spring, cats shed a lot to get rid of their thick winter fur.

Cats can twist to clean every part of their fur.

This kitten has wet its paw with its tongue and is using it like a face cloth.

Usually cats keep themselves very clean and don't need baths.

Keeping cool

In hot weather your cat may wash its fur more often. This is like having a shower to cool down. It may also lie stretched out, so that more air can reach its skin.

For links to websites, go to
www.usborne-quicklinks.com
and enter the keywords "first pets cats".

Keeping fur healthy

When your cat washes, it swallows loose fur which can make it sick. You can help your cat to get rid of loose fur by brushing it regularly.

Relax your cat by stroking it, before you start brushing.

Cat brushes

1. Brush your cat at least once a week. Long-haired cats may need brushing more often.

2. Get an old towel or blanket for your cat to stand on. Sit your cat on your lap or on a table.

Brush the fur in the direction it grows.

Don't brush near its eyes.

Only brush your cat's stomach if it likes it.

3. Start by brushing its back, then its legs and tail. Brush your cat under its chin and around its ears.

4. Some cats don't like being brushed at all. Try to get your kitten used to being brushed while it's still young.

Shades for hiding

In the wild, cats have fur shades that match the places where they live. Tigers have stripes on their fur which look like the long grass that they hide in.

Domestic cats come in lots of different shades too. Where could your cat hide best?

Paws and Claws

In the wild, cats use their claws to catch food and to protect themselves. Your cat uses its paws to explore. It uses its claws to dig into things, such as trees, so that it can climb them.

Scratching signs

As your cat scratches, it files its claws to keep them sharp. The scratches also show other cats that it has been there.

Scent glands on your cat's paws leave a smell where it scratches.

When it scratches, your cat leaves its smell behind as a sign to mark its territory.

Claws are made of keratin, like your fingernails.

Walk like a cat

Cats swing their paws in front of each other as they walk, as if they are walking along a line. This means that they can easily walk along narrow ledges and fences. Try walking like your cat.

Your footprints show a gap between your feet.

Fur between its toes helps a cat to walk very quietly.

This kitten taps a strange toy with its paws to see if it is safe.

For links to websites, go to
www.usborne-quicklinks.com
and enter the keywords "first pets cats".

Scratching posts

Outside, your cat will use a tree to sharpen its claws. Inside, if your cat tries to scratch the furniture, you need to buy a scratching post and train it to use it.

All cats need somewhere to scratch. If you see your kitten scratching the furniture, say "No!" in a firm voice. Take it to its scratching post.

A scratching post has rough rope or carpet around it.

Train your cat by lifting its paw up and down gently against the post.

All about claws

There are four toes on each of your cat's front paws and one small toe higher up its leg, a bit like a thumb. This is called a dew claw.

Cats like to stretch up, like this kitten, when they scratch.

Cats put out their claws when they want to scratch.

Your cat's claws are pulled in most of the time. This stops them from being worn away too quickly.

Training

As your kitten grows up, it will need to learn what it can and can't do in your house. Your kitten will learn faster if you teach it while it is still young. Use your kitten's name when you're training it. It will start to recognize its name the more you use it. Praise your kitten when it does something that you want it to.

Litter tray training

It may have forgotten where its litter tray is.

Wear rubber gloves and wash your hands after emptying the tray.

When your kitten has finished eating, pick it up and put it in its litter tray. Leave your kitten to go to the toilet on his own.

If you see your kitten crouching down with its tail up, pick it up. Quickly take it to its litter tray so that it can go to the toilet.

Empty the litter tray every day. Put the dirty litter into a plastic bag and throw it away. Refill the tray and put it on old newspapers.

Most kittens will have learned how to use a litter tray from their mother.

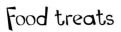

For links to websites, go to
www.usborne-quicklinks.com
and enter the keywords "first pets cats".

Food treats

When you're training your kitten and it does what you want it to, give it something to eat as a treat.

Most cats will like a teaspoon of yogurt or a small piece of cheese as a treat. They may also like a small piece of cooked meat or fish, but remember to pull out all the bones. Don't give your cat any leftovers or chocolate. These can make your cat very ill.

Training your kitten

Never hit your cat.

When you see your kitten doing something it shouldn't, say its name and "No!" in a firm voice.

Your kitten will want to explore. Don't let it onto surfaces where food is prepared and eaten.

Remember to praise your cat when it does something good. Stroke it and give it a treat.

Find out which treat your cat likes best.

Cat language

Some cats like to meow a lot to tell you how they feel. Using different meows, your cat will tell you if it's hungry or wants attention. Watch the way your cat moves to find out what it is saying to you.

Your cat might arch its back, like this kitten, when it says "hello".

Feeling happy

A cat sways its tail gently when it is happy.

Your cat shows that it is pleased to see you by putting its tail straight up. Its ears point to the front. It might also make a chirruping noise to say "hello".

When it is happy, your cat makes a rumbling sound called a purr. It makes the noise deep in its throat as it breathes. Stroking your cat usually makes it purr.

Feeling safe

When your cat rolls over and shows you its stomach, it trusts you. Your cat will probably not do this if there is someone nearby that it does not know.

Only stroke your cat's stomach if it likes it.

For links to websites, go to
www.usborne-quicklinks.com
and enter the keywords "first pets cats".

Feeling angry

When a cat is angry,
it twitches its tail and its
ears point back. The
black part of its eyes, the
pupils, grow wider. Leave
your cat alone if it looks
annoyed.

*An angry
cat may also
hiss or spit.*

*When a cat is angry or
scared, it flattens
its ears.*

*Cats fluff up
their fur like this
to make them
look bigger.*

*It may put
its claws out,
ready to fight.*

Mixed messages

*This kitten's ears are pointing to
the front to show that it's happy,
but its fur is fluffed up.*

Sometimes, when a cat is
playing, it mixes signs that it
is happy or angry. It may fluff up
its fur but point its ears to the front.

21

Staying healthy

As your kitten grows up, you'll need to take it to the vet. It is a good idea to take your cat to the vet at least once a year, even if it is not ill. The vet can check that your cat is healthy.

Watch out for signs of your cat going off its food or looking scruffy. If you are worried, find the number of your nearest vet in a telephone directory. Ask the vet for advice before taking your cat in. Visiting a vet can be expensive.

Going to the vet

Put a blanket around it.

Take your cat to the vet if it becomes ill. Keep it warm and stay quiet when you're nearby, so that it can rest.

Leave it in its carrier until the vet is ready to see you.

Pick your cat up carefully and put it into its pet carrier. Put it into the carrier bottom first.

Twelve weeks old

At twelve weeks old your kitten will need to have some injections.

You'll need to take your kitten to a vet when you first get it. The vet will check that your kitten is healthy and give it some injections.

Six months old

At six months old, your kitten can be neutered. This is an operation which stops it from having kittens or being the father of kittens.

Every year

Your cat will need extra injections from your vet every year. This is to make sure it is still protected against diseases.

For links to websites, go to
www.usborne-quicklinks.com
and enter the keywords **"first pets cats"**.

Fleas and tapeworms

*Fleas
live
in fur.*

*A cat might
eat more if it has
tapeworms.*

Even if your cat is very clean, it may have fleas living on it. If you see your cat scratching a lot, it may have fleas. Use a special spray from a vet to get rid of them.

Tapeworms can live in a cat's stomach. If you see something like a grain of rice near its bottom, your cat may have tapeworms. Don't touch them, but tell an adult.

Getting older

Cats can live for 14 years or longer. As your cat gets older, it may find it more difficult to stretch around to clean its fur. Help your cat keep clean by brushing it more often.

*Older cats will sit
and sleep more.*

*Let your cat sit in a
warm, quiet place.*

Going outside

Kittens and cats love to explore outside. If you do not have an area outside where your cat can go, it will need enough space to exercise inside and a sunny place to sit. Your cat can go outside two weeks after it has had its injections. Put an elasticated cat collar with an identity tag on your cat in case it gets lost.

The elastic on a collar stretches if it catches on something and lets your cat escape.

Out and about

Make sure your cat is wearing a collar before you let it explore on its own. When you fit the collar, make sure you can easily get two fingers under it.

When you want your cat to come inside, call its name. Crouch down and hold out your hand. Your cat may come if it hears you shaking a box of cat food.

Write your telephone number on the tag.

24

For links to websites, go to
www.usborne-quicklinks.com
and enter the keywords "first pets cats".

Cat flap training

A cat flap is a small door for your cat. It allows your cat to go outside and come back inside when it likes. Some cat flaps have locks on them so that you can keep your cat inside. Don't lock your cat outside at night.

Only leave a cat flap propped open, like this, when you are training. You don't want other cats coming into your house.

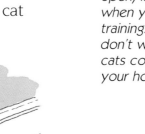

1. Prop the cat flap open with a ruler or stick. Tempt your cat through it with a food treat or a toy.

Try pulling some string through for it to chase.

2. After your cat has gone through its cat flap, go to the other side and call it through again.

Push the flap gently so that you don't scare your cat.

3. Take away the prop when your cat is through the flap. Push the flap to show your cat how it works.

4. Let your cat push through the flap a few times. Your cat will soon get used to using it.

Hunting and fighting

What do you think your cat gets up to without you? When your cat is outside, it may meet other cats and explore its territory. It may look for small animals to hunt. Cats sometimes like to bring home the things that they catch.

Play fighting

As kittens play together, they learn how to defend their territory. Kittens often look as if they are fighting and may even hiss or spit. They won't hurt each other, as their fur protects them from sharp claws.

Sharing territories

There is often one cat who is the boss in a territory.

Cats may share a territory, but there is always one who is the leader. If you hear cats making loud wailing noises, they may be fighting over which one is the leader. The loser might creep away, very slowly.

The kittens in this picture are play fighting.

Even when kittens are playing, they make themselves look as big and fierce as they can.

For links to websites, go to
www.usborne-quicklinks.com
and enter the keywords "first pets cats".

Hunting

Even well-fed cats like to hunt. When a cat sees something to catch, it stays very still then moves slowly closer. Its whiskers and ears point to the front and it watches very carefully. Just before a cat pounces it may wiggle its bottom.

This cat's tail twitches, just as it is about to pounce.

Perched in a high place, this kitten may wait for a long time to pounce on something.

In the dark

In dim light, your cat sees objects five times brighter than you can. This makes it easy for cats to move around at night without bumping into things.

Pouncing on toys is good practice for hunting.

In total darkness cats use their whiskers to feel when objects are close. The animals that cats hunt cannot see as well in the dark as they can.

Cats and plants

You may see your cat trying to nibble at plants. It is best not to let your cat eat any plants except grass and catnip. There are some plants that are poisonous to cats.

Eating grass

Chewing houseplants

Some houseplants, such as these, are poisonous.

Crocus   *Poinsettia*   *Hyacinth*

If you see your cat chewing a houseplant, say "No!", firmly. Put pieces of orange or lemon peel in the plant pot. Most cats don't like the smell of peel.

Your cat may also like some grass to chew on. You could grow some grass in a pot for your cat. Some experts say that eating grass helps cats to vomit to get rid of any fur they may have swallowed.

This silver tabby cat is rubbing its head against a catnip plant.

For links to websites, go to
www.usborne-quicklinks.com
and enter the keywords "first pets cats".

Catnip

A lot of cats like a plant called catnip, or catmint. Kittens are able to smell catnip when they are six months old. They like to rub against it and chew it. Some toys have dried catnip inside. You can buy this from a pet store, or grow it and dry it yourself.

How to dry catnip

Catnip takes about a week to dry.

Tie some catnip together and hang it upside-down in a paper bag. Put the bag in a warm, dry place.

When the leaves crumble in your fingers, take them out. You can now use them to stuff a toy for your cat.

Catnip toy

Don't make the tail too thin.

1. Draw a fish shape on some thin paper. Make it about 10cm (4in) long and 5cm (2in) wide.

2. Pin the fish to some felt. Carefully cut around the shape twice. Pin the two pieces together.

3. Sew around the edges using small stitches. Leave a big gap on the bottom edge for the filling.

Draw on eyes with a felt-tip pen.

Squeeze the fish to make the catnip smell come out.

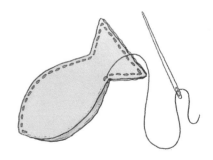

4. Push a piece of a cotton ball into the fish. Add some catnip, more of the cotton ball and sew up the gap.

Going away

If you go away overnight you will need someone else to look after your cat. Some cats like to travel, but most prefer to stay at home where they feel safe. It is best not to leave your kitten alone overnight until it is at least 4 months old and is settled into your home.

Very young kittens do not like to be left alone.

Give your cat lots of attention before you go out.

Cat hotels

Your cat's blanket will remind it of your home.

When you go away, your cat can stay in a special boarding house for cats. Take your cat's blanket to the boarding house. All the other things it needs will be provided.

Home comforts

Most cats don't like changes so will prefer to stay at home when you go away. Ask a friend to visit every day to feed your cat and empty its litter tray.

If your cat is old enough, ask your friend to let it out for a short time then call it in. If you have a cat flap, leave it unlocked so that your cat can go out when it likes.

Moving

For links to websites, go to
www.usborne-quicklinks.com
and enter the keywords "first pets cats".

If you move to a new house, pack your cat's litter tray, cat litter, food, food dishes and some toys all together. Make sure you can get to these things easily. Your cat will need them as soon as you arrive. When you are ready to leave your old home, put a small food treat inside a pet carrier and lift your cat into it. It is not a good idea to let your cat out of its carrier while you travel to your new home.

Take all the things your cat usually needs.

Let your cat play in its carrier for several days before you move.

This pet carrier has gaps in the sides so that the cat can see out.

Packing and moving will seem very strange to your cat. Keep it inside for a few days before you move and give it lots of extra attention.

Give it some water and food as soon as you arrive.

When you arrive, open the pet carrier and let your cat explore its new home. Keep your cat inside for at least a week, until it has settled in.

INDEX

With thanks:
Cecilia Keating, Olivia Lowes and Sam Perry